Mongol Warriors

by Brian Dittmar

BELLWETHER MEDIA · MINNEAPOLIS, MN

Are you ready to take it to the extreme?
Torque books thrust you into the action-packed world
of sports, vehicles, mystery, and adventure. These books
may include dirt, smoke, fire, and dangerous stunts.
Warning: read at your own risk.

Library of Congress Cataloging-in-Publication Data

Dittmar, Brian.
 Mongol warriors / by Brian Dittmar.
     p. cm. -- (Torque: History's greatest warriors)
 Includes bibliographical references and index.
 Summary: "Engaging images accompany information about Mongol warriors. The combination of
high-interest subject matter and light text is intended for students in grades 3 through 7"--Provided by
publisher.
 Audience: Grades 3-7.
 ISBN 978-1-60014-746-3 (hbk. : alk. paper)
 1. Mongols--History--Juvenile literature. 2. Mongols--Warfare--Juvenile literature. 3. Military art and
science--Mongolia--History--To 1500--Juvenile literature. I. Title.
 DS19.D557 2012
 950'.2--dc23   2011029086

This edition first published in 2012 by Bellwether Media, Inc.

Contents

Who Were Mongol Warriors?

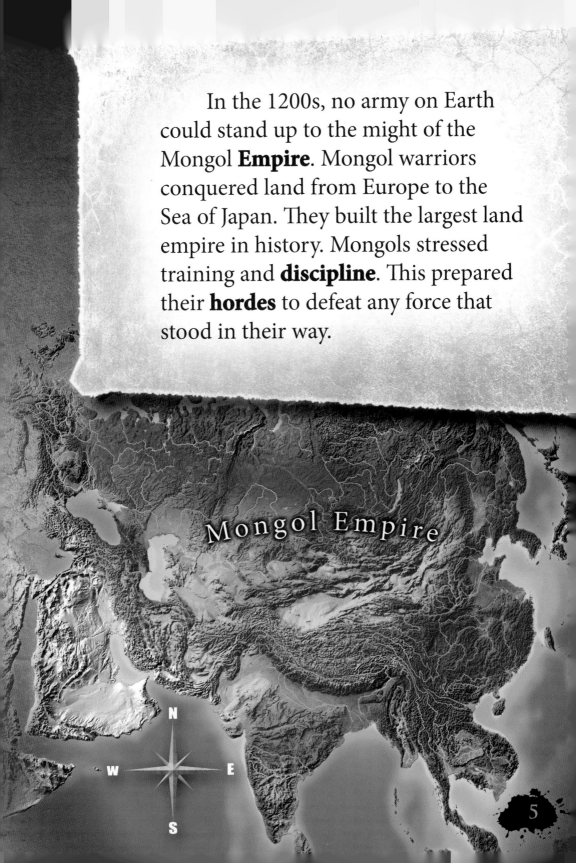

In the 1200s, no army on Earth could stand up to the might of the Mongol **Empire**. Mongol warriors conquered land from Europe to the Sea of Japan. They built the largest land empire in history. Mongols stressed training and **discipline**. This prepared their **hordes** to defeat any force that stood in their way.

Mongol Empire

N
W   E
S

The **khan** led the Mongol armies into battle. Groups of warriors attacked in waves. The **vanguard** charged into battle first. Its job was to create panic among the enemy forces. Then **cavalry** surrounded the opposing force. **Infantry** and more cavalry swept in to finish off the enemy.

Mongol Fact

Genghis Khan united many central Asian tribes in 1206. He led them into battle and built the vast Mongol Empire.

Mongol Warrior
Training

Mongol warriors started to train when they were very young. All Mongol warriors perfected the bow and arrow. They also needed to be expert horsemen. Mongol boys grew up herding on horseback and hunting with bows and arrows. This gave them the skills they would use as warriors.

Mongol Fact

The Mongols believed that much of their strength came from their ancestors.

Mongol warriors advanced in rank based on **merit**. Some warriors chose their own leaders. The khan chose his commanders based on their combat abilities. This kept Mongol armies strong and organized. Warriors believed in their commanders. Their trust in their leaders helped the hordes claim victory.

Mongol Warrior Equipment

composite bow

The **composite bow** was the most important Mongol weapon. It was small, powerful, and could be easily fired from horseback. Mongol **bowyers** also made large composite bows. These bows fired arrows with incredible force.

Warriors used a variety of arrows with their bows. Howler arrows made a whistling sound as they sailed through the air. This struck fear into enemies. Sharp, double-edged arrows could pierce enemy armor. Some warriors lit special arrows on fire before launching them into the air.

Mongol Fact

A Mongol archer carried several quivers. Each quiver held up to 30 arrows.

Warriors also fought with swords, spears, and axes. The most common hand-to-hand Mongol weapon was the saber. A warrior could **wield** this curved sword both on the ground and on horseback.

Mongols needed armor for warmth and protection. They wore a long coat called a *khatangu degel*. Leather armor with light metal plates went over this coat. Warriors also wore metal-plated boots and helmets with face guards. Many carried leather shields as well. Silk clothing under their armor helped keep arrows from piercing their skin.

Mongol Fact

Many Mongol warriors had several horses in reserve. This way they never had to ride a tired horse.

Mongol Units

Mongol armies were organized into groups based on the number 10.

10 soldiers formed an *arban*

10 *arban* formed a *jaghun* (100 soldiers)

10 *jaghun* formed a *mingghan* (1,000 soldiers)

10 *mingghan* formed a *tjumen* (10,000 soldiers)

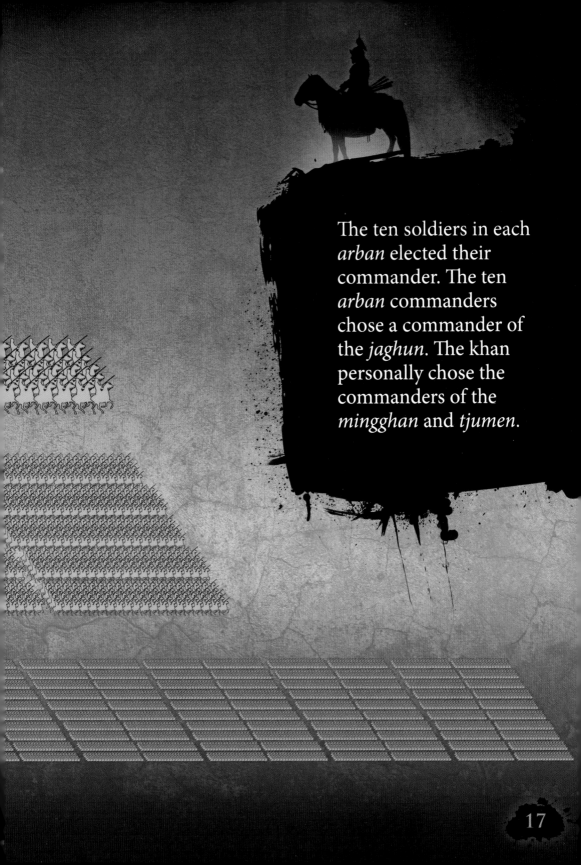

The ten soldiers in each *arban* elected their commander. The ten *arban* commanders chose a commander of the *jaghun*. The khan personally chose the commanders of the *mingghan* and *tjumen*.

The Decline of Mongol Warriors

Ilkhanate

From 1206 to 1259, Genghis Khan and his relatives led a united Mongol Empire. His grandson Möngke Khan died in 1259. The remaining relatives fought over who should rule. The empire split into four **independent** parts.

Khanate of the
Golden Horde

Khanate of the
Great Khan

Chagatai
Khanate

N
W   E
S

19

The four parts of the Mongol Empire remained powerful for more than 100 years. Some even conquered other lands. Eventually they were all overtaken by greater powers. The feared Mongol hordes and their mighty empire had faded away.

Mongol Fact

The last of the four separate empires was the Chagatai Khanate, which fell in 1658.

Glossary

bowyers—people who make bows

cavalry—military troops on horseback

composite bow—a type of bow that creates a lot of tension and power; the Mongol composite bow was far more powerful than those used by other armies.

discipline—order and control

empire—a kingdom made up of many lands

hordes—large groups of warriors or people

independent—free from the control of others

infantry—soldiers on foot

khan—a leader of the Mongols

merit—the quality of being worthy

vanguard—the group that leads an army into battle

wield—to handle effectively

To Learn More

AT THE LIBRARY

Burgan, Michael. *Empire of the Mongols*. New York, N.Y.: Chelsea House, 2009.

Kent, Zachary. *Genghis Khan: Invincible Ruler of the Mongol Empire*. Berkeley Heights, N.J.: Enslow Publishers, Inc., 2008.

Streissguth, Thomas. *Genghis Khan's Mongol Empire*. Farmington Hills, Mich.: Lucent Books, 2006.

ON THE WEB

Learning more about Mongol warriors is as easy as 1, 2, 3.

1. Go to www.factsurfer.com.

2. Enter "Mongol warriors" into the search box.

3. Click the "Surf" button and you will see a list of related Web sites.

With factsurfer.com, finding more information is just a click away.

Index

Great care has been taken to select images that are both historically accurate and engaging. The depictions of the warriors in this book may vary slightly due to the use of images from multiple sources and reenactments.